WORD by WORD

PRIMARY
PHONICS PICTURE DICTIONARY

Steven J. Molinsky • Bill Bliss

Illustrated by

Richard E. Hill

Maya Shorr Katz

LONGMAN

INTRODUCTION

The *Word by Word Primary Phonics Picture Dictionary* program offers a systematic, phonics-based curriculum presenting over 1000 words through lively and motivating illustrations. The program provides a comprehensive introduction to sound/letter association, phonograms (word families), decoding and word recognition, and vocabulary concepts and skills. While the program is designed for effective use by all children, its picture-based instruction and careful curriculum sequence are particularly appropriate for English language learners and other special needs students studying in school, small-group, tutorial, and family learning settings.

The program consists of the core Primary Phonics Picture Dictionary, Workbooks at three levels (Grades K, 1–2, and 3–4), an Audio Program, Picture/Word Cards, a Song Album, a Teacher's Guide, and a Tutor's Handbook. These materials are designed to serve as a teacher's main resource for that portion of instructional time devoted to systematic, explicit phonics-based instruction. Frequent, short phonics-based lessons (perhaps 10–15 minutes) are recommended as an adjunct to other ongoing reading and language instruction.

TEACHING STRATEGIES

The core learning device in the dictionary is a lesson consisting of words and pictures accompanied by an illustrated phrase or sentence at the bottom of the page. Specific teaching strategies vary in each unit and are covered in the Teacher's Guide. Some general suggestions are:

<u>Introduce the Lesson:</u> Tell children the lesson objective using simple language (such as "word families") rather than technical terms (such as "phonograms").

<u>Present the Words:</u> (For Unit 2, first use the appropriate Picture/Word Cards to build phonemic awareness through aural/oral practice in *segmenting* and *blending* sounds. Point to a picture, say each sound of the word separately, and have children repeat and practice. Then model how the sounds blend to make the word and have children repeat and practice.) For all units, say each word as children look at the word and picture in the dictionary and then have children repeat the word chorally and individually. Say the word again slowly and have children practice *tracking* aurally by pointing to each letter as its sound is heard. Then have children practice blending as they read each word aloud.

<u>Discuss Word Meanings and Pictures:</u> For each word, have children describe what they see in the picture. Talk about the context and extend vocabulary as appropriate. Ask questions such as, "What color is the fruit?" or "Why do you think he's angry?"

<u>Analyze and Practice Word Structures:</u> Say each word and have children count and identify the separate sounds (and later, syllables) that make up the word. On the board, write the word with extra space or a plus sign between each letter or combination of letters that represents a separate sound. Have children practice *tracking* by pointing to the letter(s) that represent a sound as you say each word slowly. Have them practice *blending* by saying the words aloud, smoothly combining the separate sounds to form each word.

<u>Make Sentences:</u> Have children think of sentences for each word and share them orally (not in writing).

<u>Spelling Partners:</u> Have children work in pairs to check each other's ability to spell the words in the lesson.

<u>The Illustrated Phrase or Sentence:</u> Have children look at the illustration and talk about the characters, setting, and situation. Read the phrase or sentence slowly and have children practice *tracking* each separate word. Then have children practice reading aloud. Have fun with the illustrations and use them for discussions, role-play skits, and prompts for original student artwork or writing.

<u>Spelling & Dictation Quiz:</u> Use the words for spelling homework and quizzes based on these predictable letter-sound associations.

<u>Supplementary Practice:</u> The Workbooks provide activities for writing, listening, and reading decodable text. The Audio Program and the Song Album provide valuable listening/reading and singing practice.

<u>Expansion:</u> Have students bring in magazine photos of vocabulary words and create wall posters for each lesson. This and other activities are suggested in the Teacher's Guide.

We hope that the *Word by Word Primary Phonics Picture Dictionary* program helps you create for your students a phonics-based learning experience that is effective, interactive, responsive to students' different strengths and learning styles . . . and fun!

Steven J. Molinsky
Bill Bliss

Library of Congress Cataloging-in-Publication Data

Molinsky, Steven J.
    Word by word primary phonics picture dictionary / Steven J. Molinsky, Bill Bliss ; illustrated by Richard E. Hill, Maya Shorr Katz.
      p.   cm.
    Summary: A phonics-based presentation of over 1000 English words through illustrations, including an introduction to phonemic awareness, decoding and word recognition, and vocabulary concepts and skills development.
    ISBN 0-13-022206-2. -- ISBN 0-13-022171-6 (pbk.)
    1. Picture dictionaries, English Juvenile literature.
    [1. Picture dictionaries.] I. Bliss, Bill. II. Hill, Richard E., PE1629.M584 2000
    423'.1--dc21
                                    99-15215
                                           CIP

Editorial Director: *Louise Jennewine*
Executive Editor: *Anne Stribling*
Director of Design and Production: *Rhea Banker*
Associate Director of Electronic Publishing: *Aliza Greenblatt*
Production/Editorial Design Manager: *Paul Belfanti*
Production Manager: *Ray Keating*
Senior Manufacturing Manager: *Patrice Fraccio*
Manufacturing Buyer: *Dave Dickey*
Electronic Production Editors, Page Compositors, Interior Designers:
  Paula Williams, Wendy Wolf
Cover Designer: *Merle Krumper*

Cover Artists: *Richard E. Hill, Maya Shorr Katz, Carey Davies*
Scanners, Color Correctors: *Todd D. Ware, Robert W. Handago*
Production Assistant: *Robert Siek*
Manuscript Preparation Assistant: *Rose Ann Merrey*
Illustrations: *Richard E. Hill, Maya Shorr Katz*

Word by Word Primary Phonics Picture Dictionary
© 2000 by PEARSON EDUCATION.

Pearson Education, 10 Bank St., White Plains, NY 10606

Paperback ISBN 0-13-022171-6
Hardback ISBN 0-13-022206-2

Printed in the United States of America

20 19 18 17 16 15 14 13 12

> **Note:**
> Kindergarten-level lessons are in Units 1 & 2
> and on pages 74, 80, 180–185.

ALPHABET
&
CONCEPTS ABOUT PRINT

Alphabet

Uppercase Print
Lowercase Print
Uppercase Type
Lowercase Type

Concepts About Print

Top, Bottom, Left, Right
Letter, Word, Sentence, Page

A B C D E

F G H I J

K L M N O

P Q R S T

U V W X Y Z

a b c d e

f g h i j

k l m n o

p q r s t

u v w x y z

A B C D E

F G H I J

K L M N O

P Q R S T

U V W X Y Z

a b c d e

f g h i j

k l m n o

p q r s t

u v w x y z

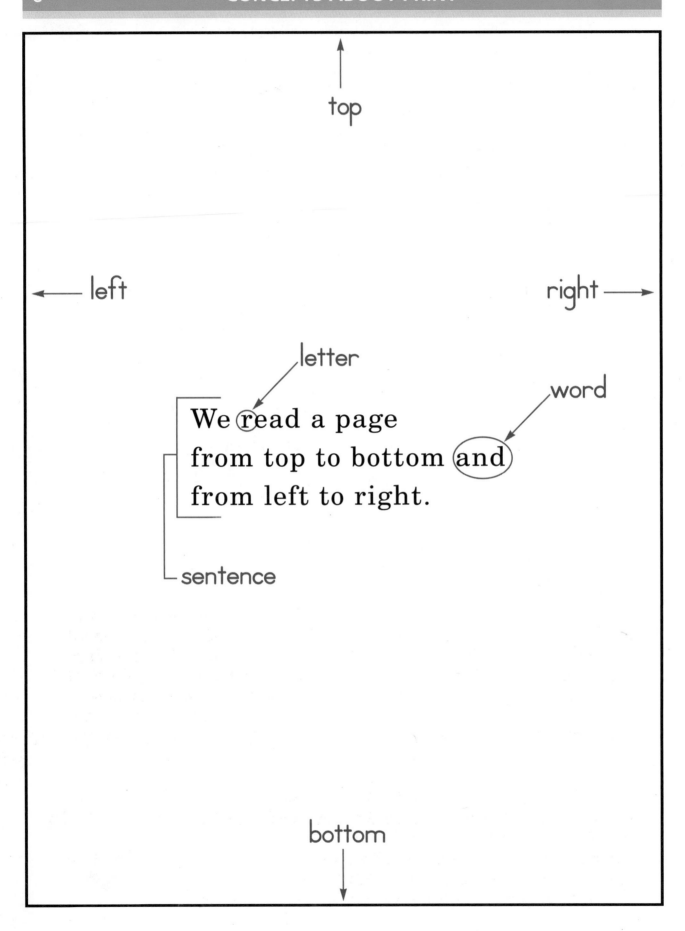

top

left

right

letter

word

We read a page
from top to bottom and
from left to right.

sentence

bottom

UNIT 2

SOUND/LETTER ASSOCIATION & PHONOGRAMS

Initial Consonants & Short Vowel Word Families

m, v + an   *p, w, f + in*
c, p + an   *l, f, h + og*
m, c, b + at   *c, p, h + ot*
m, c, l + ap   *m, h, t + en*
p, b, w + ig   *p, n, g + et*
p, s, k + it   *b, r, s + un*
d, r, z + ip   *m, b, j, + ug*

Short Vowel Word Families (Mixed Initial Consonants)

an   *ot*
ap   *og, op*
at   *et*
ad   *en*
ag, am   *ug*
ig   *un, ut*
ip   *ub, up, ud*
it

Initial Short Vowels

a, e, i, o, u

Blending Initial Consonants, Mixed Short Vowels, & Mixed Final Consonants

m + Short Vowel + Consonant   *l* + Short Vowel + Consonant
n + Short Vowel + Consonant   *b* + Short Vowel + Consonant
f + Short Vowel + Consonant   *p* + Short Vowel + Consonant
s + Short Vowel + Consonant   *d* + Short Vowel + Consonant
h + Short Vowel + Consonant   *t* + Short Vowel + Consonant
j + Short Vowel + Consonant   *g* + Short Vowel + Consonant
r + Short Vowel + Consonant   *c, k* + Short Vowel + Consonant

Review & Expansion

Consonants and Short Vowels: Review Chart with Pictures
Consonants and Short Vowels: Review Chart with Words
Rhyming Words
Changes in Words: Vowel Substitutions
Changes in Words: Consonant Substitutions
Changes in Words: Consonant & Vowel Substitutions

an

m + a + n  man

v + a + n  van

man   van

a man in a van

an

c + a + n  can

p + a + n  pan

can   pan

a can and a pan

at

m + a + t   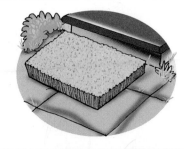   mat

c + a + t   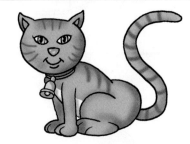   cat

b + a + t      bat

mat   cat   bat

a cat and a bat

ap

m + a + p      map

c + a + p      cap

l + a + p      lap

map   cap   lap

a cap on a lap

ig

p + i + g      pig

b + i + g      big

w + i + g      wig

pig   big   wig

a big pig in a wig

it

p + i + t		pit
s + i + t		sit
k + i + t		kit

pit   sit   kit

sit on a pit

ip

d + i + p

dip

r + i + p

rip

z + i + p

zip

dip   rip   zip

zip and rip

in

p + i + n      pin

w + i + n      win

f + i + n      fin

pin   win   fin

a pin with a fin

og

l + o + g      log

f + o + g      fog

h + o + g      hog

log   fog   hog

a hog in the fog

c + o + t 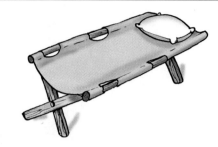 cot

p + o + t  pot

h + o + t 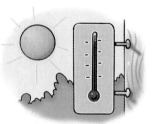 hot

cot   pot   hot

a hot pot

en

m + e + n  men

h + e + n  hen

t + e + n  ten

men　　　　hen　　　　ten

ten men and a hen

et

p + e + t  pet

n + e + t  net

g + e + t  get

pet　　　net　　　get

get a pet

un

b + u + n      bun

r + u + n      run

s + u + n      sun

bun   run   sun

   run in the sun

ug

m + u + g  mug

b + u + g 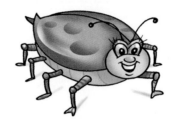 bug

j + u + g  jug

mug   bug   jug

a jug and a mug
and a bug

an

 can

 fan

 man

 pan

 ran

past tense ←

 tan

 van

can	fan	man	pan	ran	tan	van

Dan	Jan	Nan

ap

 cap

 gap

 lap

 map

 nap

 rap

 sap

 tap

cap	gap	lap	map
nap	rap	sap	tap

at

 bat

 cat

 fat

 hat

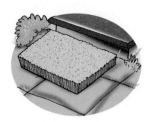 mat

 rat

 sat

 vat

bat	cat	fat	hat	mat	rat	sat	vat

Nat   Pat

ad

 bad

 dad

 lad

 mad

 pad

 sad

bad	dad	lad
mad	pad	sad

ag

 bag    rag

 tag    wag

bag   rag   tag   wag

am

 dam    ham

 jam    yam

dam   ham   jam   yam   Pam   Sam

ig

 big

 dig

 fig

 jig

 pig

 rig

 wig

| big | dig | fig | jig |

| pig | rig | wig |

ip

 dip

 hip

 lip

 rip

 sip

 tip

 zip

dip	hip	lip	rip
sip	tip	zip	

it

 bit

 fit

 hit

 kit

 lit

 pit

 sit

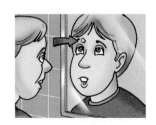 zit

bit	fit	hit	kit
lit	pit	sit	zit

ot

 cot

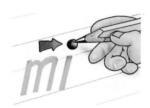 dot

got

 hot

 lot

 pot

tot

cot	dot	got	hot
lot	pot	tot	

og

 bog    fog

 hog    log

bog   fog   hog   log

op

 hop    mop

 pop    top

hop   mop   pop   top

et

 get

 jet

 met

 net

 pet

 set

 vet

 wet

get	jet	met	net
pet	set	vet	wet

en

 den

 hen

 men

 pen

 ten

den	hen	men	pen	ten
Ben		Ken		Len

ug

 bug

 dug

 hug

 jug

 mug

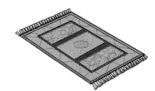 rug

 tug

bug	dug	hug	jug
mug	rug	tug	

un

 bun

 fun

 run

 sun

bun   fun   run   sun

ut

 cut

 hut

 nut

 rut

cut   hut   nut   rut

ub

 cub

 rub

 sub

 tub

cub   rub   sub   tub

up   ud

 cup

 pup

 bud

 mud

cup   pup   bud   mud

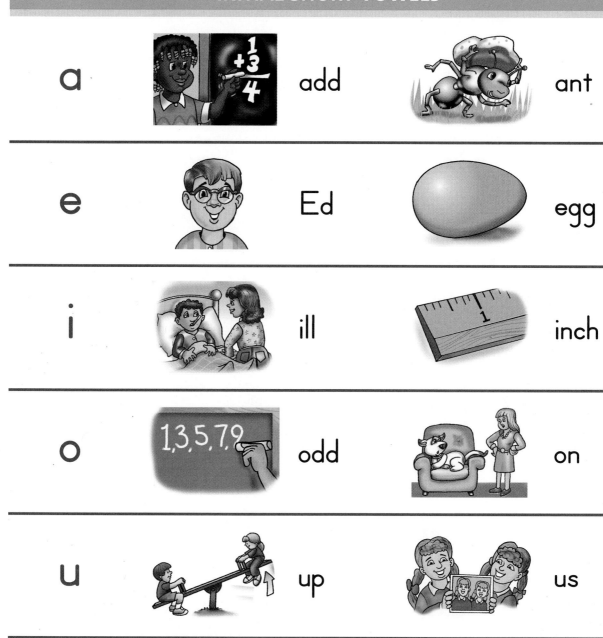

a		add	ant
e		Ed	egg
i		ill	inch
o		odd	on
u		up	us

An ant is on an egg.

a		man		mat
e		men		met
i		mill		mitt
o		mom		mop
u		mud		mug

A man with a mop is in the mill.

a  nap ·  Nat

e  net ·  neck

i  nit ·  Nick

o nod ·  not

u  nut

The nut is in the net.

a      fan      fat

e      fed      fell

i      fig      fin

o      fog

u      fun

The fat fig fell.

a    sad    sat

e    set    sell

i    sip    sit

o    sob    sock

u    sub    sun

The sad sock
sat in the sun.

a   ham   hat

e   hem   hen

i   hip   hit

o   hog   hop

u   hug   hut

The hen hit the hog with a hat.

a  jam  Jack

e  jet  Jeff

i  jig  Jill

o  job  jog

u  jug

Jill and Jeff jog.

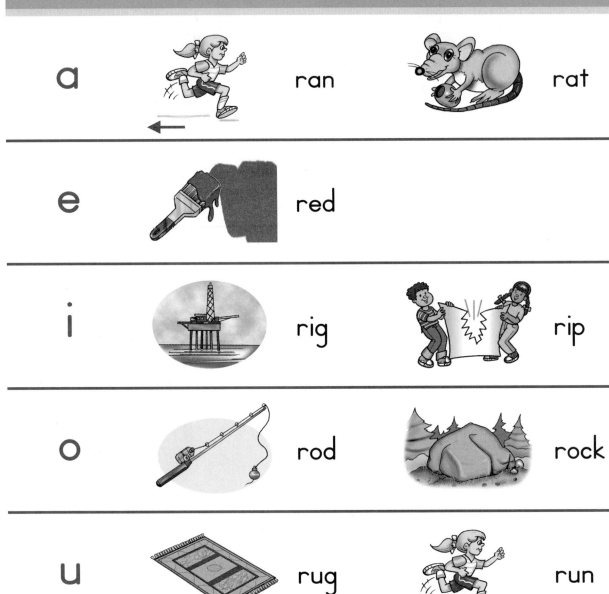

a   ran   rat

e   red

i   rig   rip

o   rod   rock

u   rug   run

The rat ran to the red rock.

a   lad   lap

e   led   leg

i   lip   lit

o   log   lot

u   luck

The lad sat on the log in the lot.

a  bag    bat

e  bed    beg

i  bib    big

o  Bob    bog

u  bug    bus

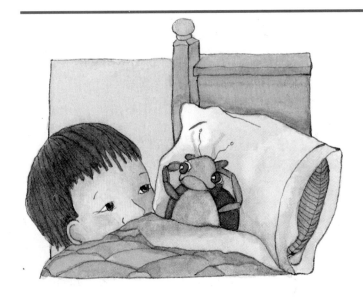

A big bug is on the bed.

a   pad   pan

e   pen   pet

i   pig   pin

o   pop   pot

u   pup

The pig and the pup
pop it with a pin.

a  dad    dam

e  den

i  dig    dip

o  dot    doll

u  dug    duck

The duck and the pup dig and dig.

a	 tag			tan
e		ten		tell
i		tip		tick
o		top		tot
u		tub		tug

The tot is in the tub with a top.

a  gap  gas

e  get

i  gill

o  got

u  gum  gull

Get gas!

a    can    cat

e   Ken

i    kid    kit

o    cod    cot

u    cub    cut

The cat is on the cot with the cub.

	a	e	i	o	u
m					
n					
f					
s					
h					
j					
r					

	a	e	i	o	u
l					
b					
p					
d					
t					
g					
c,k					

Ken

	a	e	i	o	u
m	mat	men	mitt	mop	mug
n	nap	net	nit	nod	nut
f	fan	fed	fig	fog	fun
s	sad	set	sit	sob	sun
h	hat	hen	hit	hog	hug
j	jam	jet	jig	job	jug
r	rat	red	rip	rod	rug

	a	e	i	o	u
l	lap	leg	lip	log	luck
b	bat	bed	bib	bog	bus
p	pan	pen	pig	pot	pup
d	dad	den	dig	dot	duck
t	tag	ten	tip	top	tub
g	gas	get	gill	got	gum
c,k	cat	Ken	kid	cot	cut

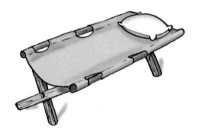

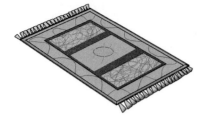

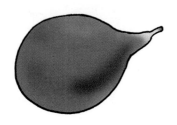

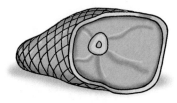  

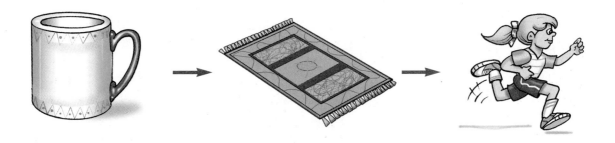

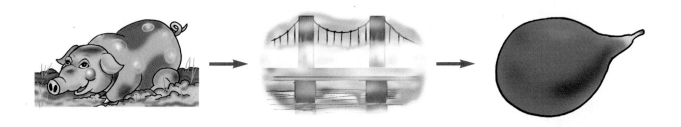

UNIT 3

DECODING & WORD RECOGNITION (1)

Initial Consonant Blends

cl, fl
cr, dr, fr, tr
sk, sl, sm, sp, st, sw

Final Consonant Blends

mp, nd, nt
lk, lt, ft
st, sk

Final Consonant *x*

Final Double Consonants

ss, ff, ll, ck

Initial Consonant *q(u)*

Initial Consonant Digraphs

sh, ch, th, wh

Final Consonant Digraphs

sh, th
ng, nk
ch, tch (Trigraph)

Review & Expansion

Distinguishing Initial & Final Sounds
Distinguishing Medial Sounds: Vocabulary Review Chart
Rhyming Words
Changes in Words: Adding Sounds
Changes in Words: Omitting Sounds
Changes in Words: Consonant & Vowel Substitutions
Changes in Words: Adding, Omitting, & Substituting Sounds

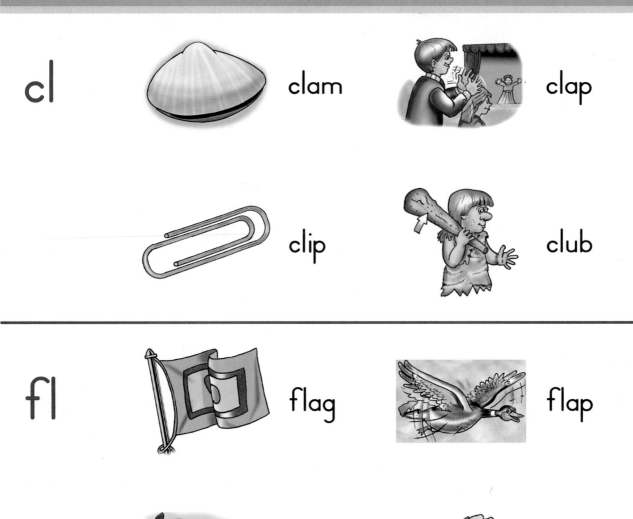

cl

clam

clap

clip

club

fl

flag

flap

flat

flip

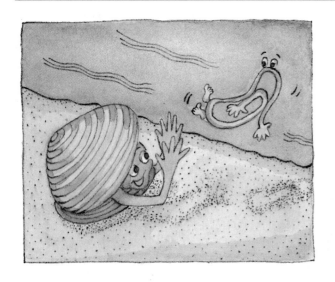

The clam can clap.
The clip can flip.

cr    crab    crop

dr    drop    drum

fr    Fran    frog

tr    trap    trot

The frog is in the
trap with the crab.

sk    skin    skip

sl    slip    slug

 sled    slot

sm    smell    smog

The slug is on the sled.

sp

 spin

 spot

st

 stem

 step

 stick

 stop

sw

 swap

 swim

Swim and get the stick!

mp    camp    lamp

 ramp    stamp

 bump    dump

 hump    jump

Jump up and sit
on the hump.

nd

 band

 hand

 sand

 stand

 bend

 mend

 wind

pond

Stand in the sand
at the pond and
bend in the wind.

nt  ant

 plant

 bent

 dent

 tent

 went

 print

 hunt

The ant went in
the tent.

lk  elk  milk

lt  belt  melt

ft  raft  left

 gift  lift

An elk with a gift is on the raft.

st

 fast

 last

 best

 nest

 rest

 test

 vest

 west

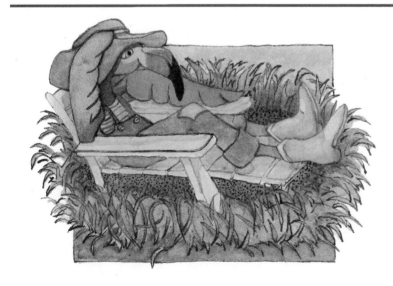

Rest in the best nest in the west.

st

 fist

 list

 dust

 crust

sk

 ask

 mask

 desk

 disk

The disk is on the desk with the mask and the list.

X

 wax

 fix

 mix

 six

 box

 fox

Fix the box with
the fox.

ss

 class

 glass

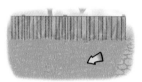 grass

 dress

 press

 kiss

ff

 cliff

 huff
puff

The class is in the
grass on the cliff.

ll

bell

fell

sell

shell

smell

spell

tell

well

yell

ill

fill

gill

hill

mill

spill

doll

gull

The doll is with the
ill gull at the well
on the hill.

ck

 back

 black

 sack

 track

 brick

 kick

 pick

 sick

 stick

 trick

 block

 clock

 lock

 rock

 sock

 duck

 luck

 truck

The duck did a trick with a block, a rock, a clock, and a black sack.

qu

 quack

 quick

 quill

 quilt

 quit

 quiz

Quack! Quack!

sh

 shell

 shelf

 shed

 ship

 shop

 shut

The shell is with the ship on the shelf in the shop.

ch

 check

 chest

 chess

 chin

 chip

 chick

 chimp

 chop

The chimp and the chick chop and chop.

th

 thank

 think

 thick

 thin

 this

 that

wh

 when

 which

"Which is thin and which is thick?"

"This is thin and that is thick."

sh

 crash

 mash

 rash

 trash

 dish

 fish

 wish

 brush

The fish in this dish is fresh.

th

 bath

 math

 path

 Beth

 Seth

 with

Beth is with Seth in math.

ng

 bang

 fang

 hang

 rang

 sang

 bring

 king

 ring

 ring

 sing

 sling

 sting

 swing

 thing

 wing

 ding dong

 ping pong

 King Kong

The king sang on the swing.

nk

 bank

 blank

 crank

 drank

 tank

 thank

 blink

 drink

 pink

 rink

 sink

 stink

 think

 wink

 bunk

 junk

 skunk

 trunk

Hank and Frank think a skunk is in the bunk.

ch  rich

 which

 ranch

 branch

 inch

 pinch

 bench

 lunch

Sit on the bench and have lunch at the ranch.

tch

 catch

 patch

 sketch

 itch

 ditch

 pitch

 switch

 Dutch

Pitch and catch in a ditch.

m   m

s   s

b   b

t   t

n   n

p   p f  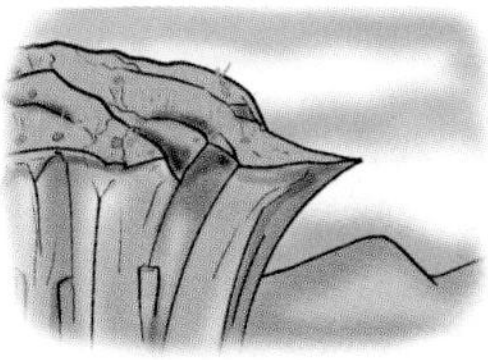   f

g     g

l  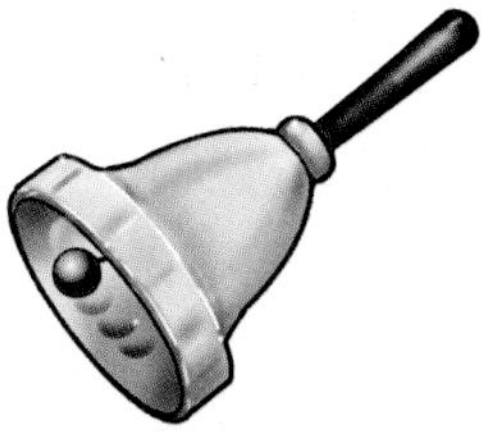   l

d  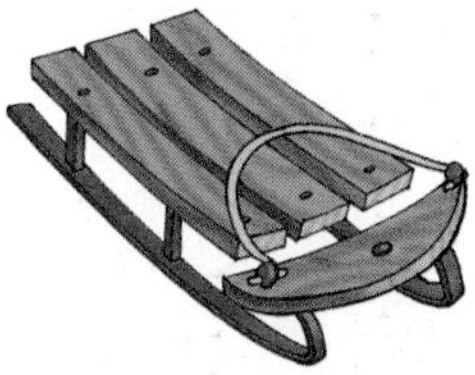   d

k     ck

ch     ch

	a	e	i	o	u
m					
n					
f					
s					
h					
j					
r					

	a	e	i	o	u
l					
b					
p					
d					
t					
g					
c, k		Ken			

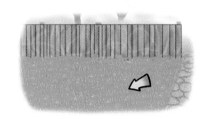

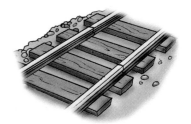

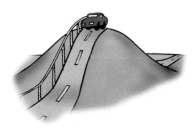

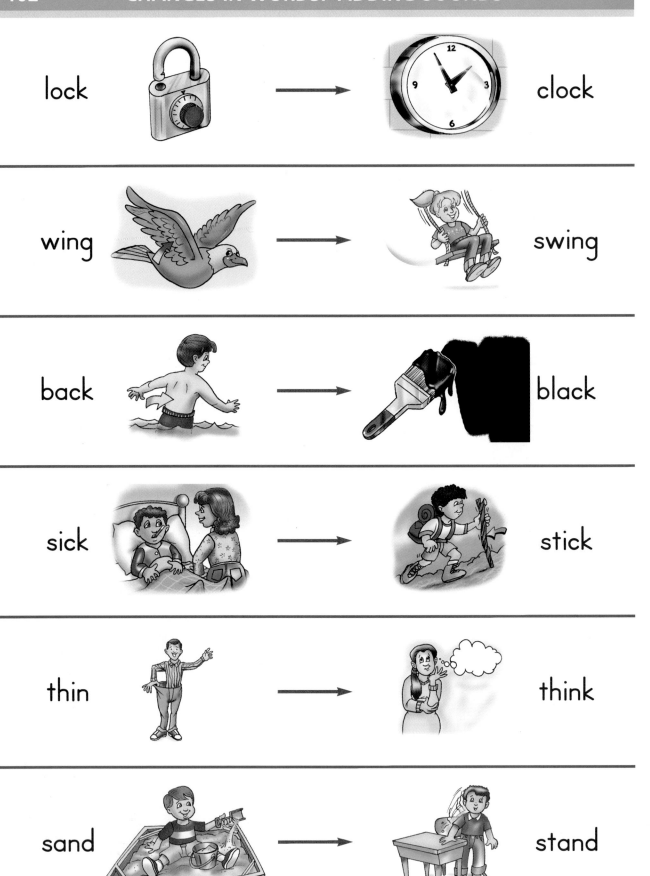

lock → clock

wing → swing

back → black

sick → stick

thin → think

sand → stand

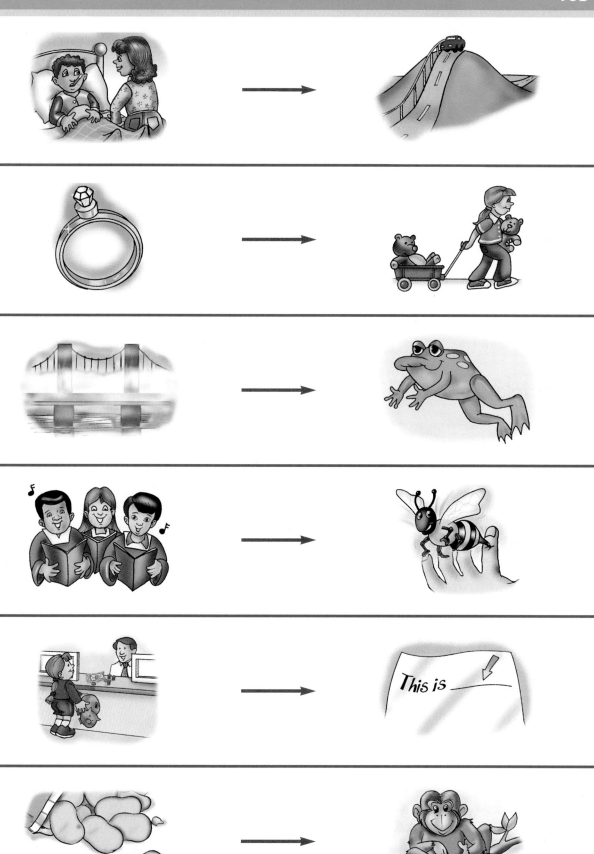

stop → top

pitch → itch

trick → tick

pinch → inch

mask → ask

crash → rash

UNIT 4

DECODING & WORD RECOGNITION (2)

Long Vowel Word Families

a□e, i□e, o□e, u□e
ee, ea
Final Long Vowels e & o
Long Vowel Word Families with ace, ice
y as a Vowel
Long Vowels with ld, ll, lt, nd
Distinguishing Short & Long Vowels

Vowel Digraphs

ay, ai
oa, oe, ow
oo, ou, ew, ue

R-Controlled Vowels

ar, ir, ur, er, or

Two-Syllable Words

Two-Syllable Words with y as a Vowel

Review & Expansion

Rhyming Words
Changes in Words

 bake

 cake

 rake

 snake

 game

 name

 cane

 lane

 mane

 plane

 cape

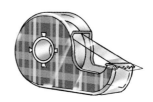 tape

 ate

 gate

 plate

 skate

 gave

 save

A snake in a cape ate the cake on a plate.

i  e

 hide

 ride

 side

 slide

 bike

 hike

 dime

 time

 nine

 pine

 pipe

 wipe

 bite

 kite

 dive

 drive

 five

 hive

The kite is in the pine with the hive.

 globe

 robe

 rode

 broke

 smoke

 hole

 mole

 pole

 stole

 dome

 home

 bone

 cone

 note

 vote

 stove

 drove

A mole in a robe is at home in a hole.

u  e

 cube

 tube

 rude

 duke

 Luke

 mule

 rule

 dune

 June

 tune

 prune

 cute

 flute

A duke with a flute
is on a cute mule
on a dune.

 man

 mane

 bit

 bite

 not

 note

 tub

 tube

 tap

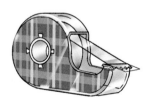 tape

ee

 bee

 see

 three

 tree

 feed

 seed

 peel

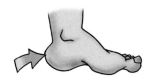 heel

 green

 queen

 jeep

 sheep

 sleep

 sweep

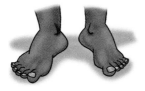 feet

 meet

 teeth

The queen is in a green jeep with three sheep.

ea

 pea

 sea

 bead

 read

 meal

 seal

 dream

 team

 bean

 clean

 eat

 beat

 meat

 seat

 peach

 teach

 leaf

 east

Eat a meal with a seal.

e

 he

 she

 me

 we

O

 go

 no

 yo-yo

ace

 brace

 face

 space

 race

ice

 ice

 mice

 rice

 slice

y

 happy

 penny

 bunny

 windy

 baby

 tiny

pony

sleepy

The tiny bunny
is sleepy.

y

cry

dry

fly

fly

fry

my

sky

why

Why did the fly cry?

ay

 clay

 day

 gray

 hay

 jay

 May

 play

 say

Kay and Jay play
with the gray clay.

ai

 rain

 train

 chain

 paint

 pail

 sail

 tail

 chair

Sail in the rain.

oa

 boat

 coat

 goat

 float

 road

 toad

 loaf

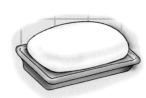 soap

oe

 hoe

 toe

ow

 bow

 blow

 crow

 grow

 low

 row

 snow

 throw

The crow and the toad throw snow at the goat in the road.

oo

 zoo

 boot

 moon

 spoon

 pool

 stool

 broom

 tooth

ou

 soup

 you

ew

 blew

 drew

 flew

 grew

 new

 threw

ue

 blue

 glue

The new blue spoon
is in the soup.

ld

 old

 cold

 fold

 gold

 hold

 sold

 told

- -

 child

 wild

ll  roll  toll

lt  bolt  colt

nd  blind  find

 kind  wind

The child and the colt find the gold.

 ar

 car

 far

 jar

 star

 card

 yard

 bark

 dark

 park

shark

 arm

 farm

 barn

 yarn

 harp

 sharp

 cart

 smart

Bark in the dark in the yard.

ir

 bird

 girl

 shirt

 skirt

 stir

 first

ur

 curl

 turn

 hurt

 church

er  herd  fern

or  fork  storm

 corn  horn

 short  north

The girl and the bird
stir the corn with a fork.

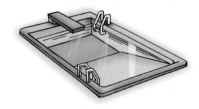

UNIT 5

DECODING & WORD RECOGNITION (3)

Vowel Diphthongs

ou, ow
oi, oy

Vowel Sounds & Spelling Patterns

aw, au, o
all
ore, oar, our, oor
oo, u
o, ea

Complex Word Families

igh, ight; ought, aught; eigh, eight

Syllabication

Medial Consonants (VCV: Vowel–Consonant–Vowel)
Double Medial Consonants (VCCV: Vowel–Consonant–Consonant–Vowel)
Different Medial Consonants (VCCV: Vowel–Consonant–Consonant–Vowel)
Two-Syllable Words with Final *le*

Silent Letters

k, w, h, l, t, b

Plural Nouns

Regular Plurals (Inflections *s, es*)
Plurals with Spelling Changes (*y* to *i*; *f* to *v*)
Irregular Plurals

Initial Consonant Blends

scr, spl, spr, str, squ

Root Words & Inflections

Verbs with Inflections *s, ed, ing*
Inflections *s, ed, ing* with Spelling Changes

Suffixes

Nouns with Suffixes *er, or*

Consonant Sounds & Spelling Patterns

Consonant *s = z*
Consonants *ph, gh = f*
Soft Consonant *g*

Common Irregular Sight Words

come, give, said, have, some, none, was, were

Review & Expansion

Rhyming Words

ou

 cloud

 shout

 round

 count

 mouth

 south

 house

 mouse

 our

 flour

ow  bow

 cow

 how

 owl

 brown

 clown

 down

 town

How did a cow, an owl, and a brown mouse get in our house?

oi

 oil

 boil

 foil

 soil

 coin

 point

oy

 boy

 toy

The boy is in the
soil with the toy.

aw    draw    saw

au    Paul    sauce

o    off    dog

 long    song

Paul saw a dog
on a long log.

all

 ball

 call

 fall

 fall

 hall

 tall

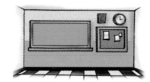 wall

 small

The small ball hit the wall in the hall.

ore  score  store

oar  oar  roar

our  four  pour

oor  door  floor

Roar at the door
in the store.

oo

 book

 brook

 cook

 hook

 look

 took

 good

 wood

 wool

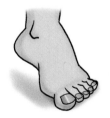 foot

u

 bull

 full

 pull

 bush

 push

 put

The bull took the wood and put it in the brook.

igh

 high

 sigh

ight

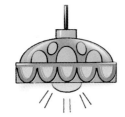 light

 night

 right

 bright

ought

 brought

 thought

aught

 caught

 taught

---

eigh

 weigh

 sleigh

---

eight

 eight

 weight

 eighty

 cabin

 camel

 wagon

 dragon

 planet

 shadow

 seven

 present

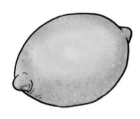 lemon

 flower

 paper

 baker

 over

 broken

 spider

 Friday

 sneaker

crayon

The wagon with the dragon is broken.

 rabbit

 ladder

 yellow

 pillow

 dollar

 follow

 hammer

 summer

 dinner

 muffin

 zipper

 puppet

 supper

 letter

 kitten

 mitten

 butter

 button

The rabbit and the kitten had a muffin with butter for dinner.

 jacket

 chicken

 doctor

 tractor

 fifteen

 fifty

 pencil

 princess

 finger

 blanket

 window

 under

 Sunday

 winter

 dirty

 sister

 father

 angry

The princess is angry at the chicken under the window.

o

 mother

 brother

 honey

 money

 Monday

 shovel

 glove

 above

 monkey

 donkey

ea  head

 bread

 thread

 heavy

 feather

 weather

 sweater

 breakfast

The monkey and the donkey eat bread with honey for breakfast.

 apple

 bubble

 middle

 puddle

 little

 puzzle

 turtle

 purple

 circle

 tickle

 needle

 steeple

 noodle

 poodle

 beetle

 eagle

 table

 cradle

The turtle and the beetle sit in the middle of a little puddle.

k

 knee

 knife

 knit

 knock

w

 wrap

 write

 wrist

 wrong

h

 white

 wheel

 wheat

 whale

l

 talk

 walk

 chalk

 calf

 half

t

 listen

 castle

b

 lamb

 comb

 climb

 thumb

 map
maps

 book
books

 seat
seats

 bike
bikes

 pen
pens

 pencil
pencils

 ruler
rulers

 globe
globes

 glass
glasses

 brush
brushes

 watch
watches

 box
boxes

y → i

penny
pennies

puppy
puppies

baby
babies

fly
flies

f → v

leaf
leaves

loaf
loaves

knife
knives

wolf
wolves

elf
elves

shelf
shelves

calf
calves

half
halves

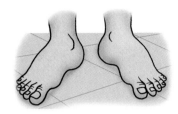 foot
feet

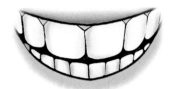 tooth
teeth

 goose
geese

 mouse
mice

 man
men

 woman
women

 child
children

 fish
fish

 sheep
sheep

 deer
deer

scr  scratch    scream

spl  splash    split

spr  spray    spring

str  straw   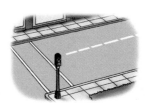 street

 stretch    string

squ  square    squirrel

	s	ed	ing
cook	cooks	cooked	cooking
work	works	worked	working
clean	cleans	cleaned	cleaning
play	plays	played	playing
brush	brushes	brushed	brushing
add	adds	added	adding

	← s →	← ed	↓ ing
study	studies y → i	studied y → i	studying
bake	bakes	baked	baking ∅
shop	shops	shopped p → pp	shopping p → pp
jog	jogs	jogged g → gg	jogging g → gg

I play. She works.
He studies.
Yesterday we shopped.
Now we're jogging.

teach
teacher

farm
farmer

sing
singer

paint
painter

act
actor

conduct
conductor

bake
baker

dance
dancer

jog
jogger

shop
shopper

swim
swimmer

win
winner

 hose

 nose

 rose

 close

 these

 those

 cheese

 choose

 please

 has

 easy

 busy

ph

 phone

 photo

 graph

 dolphin

 alphabet

 elephant

gh

 laugh

 cough

g

 giant

 giraffe

large

 orange

 come

 give

 said

 have

 some

 none

 was

 were

"Come and give me some oranges," said the giant.

"But I have none," said the elephant as he laughed.

UNIT 6

VOCABULARY &
CONCEPT DEVELOPMENT

Common Words in Basic Categories
(Identifying, Sorting, Classifying)

Colors
Shapes
Classroom Objects
Toys
Clothing
Food
Living Things (Levels of Specificity):
    Plants & Trees, Birds, Insects, Animals, People

Root Words & Inflections

Adjectives with *er, est*

Synonyms

Antonyms

Multiple Meaning Words

Homonyms (Same Sound, Same Spelling)
Homographs (Same Spelling, Different Sounds)

Homophones

(Different Meanings & Spellings, Same Sound)

Simple Prefixes & Suffixes

un–, re–, dis–; –ly, –ful, –less

Compound Words

Multisyllabic Words

Review & Expansion

Multisyllabic Word Game (Classifying & Syllabication)

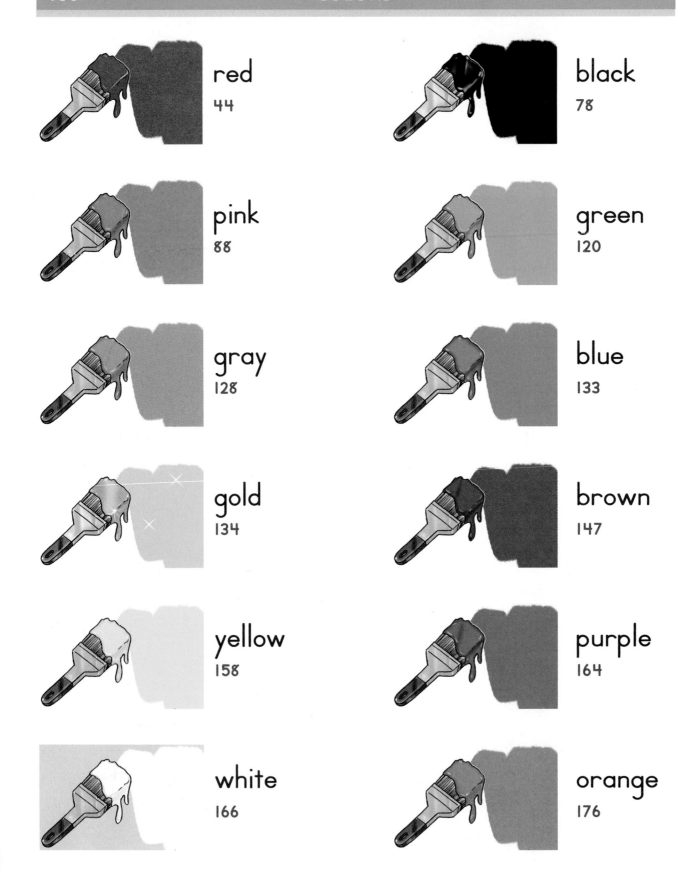

red
44

black
78

pink
88

green
120

gray
128

blue
133

gold
134

brown
147

yellow
158

purple
164

white
166

orange
176

The number indicates the page on which the word first appears. If a student has difficulty decoding or recognizing a word, refer to that page for more practice.

 circle

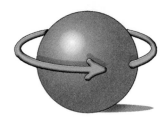 round

 triangle

 rectangle

 square

 oval

"What do you see?"

"I see a yellow circle, five green triangles, a pink square, and a brown rectangle. And you?"

"I see a girl sitting on a bench in a park on a sunny day."

Classroom Objects

desk
73

globe
114

chair
129

book
152

paper
157

crayon
157

pencil
160

chalk
167

Toys

doll
77

yo-yo
124

The number indicates the page on which the word first appears. If a student has difficulty decoding or recognizing a word, refer to that page for more practice.

Clothing

cap
11

hat
24

dress
75

coat
130

boot
132

shirt
138

skirt
138

sneaker
157

mitten
159

jacket
160

glove
162

sweater
163

Food

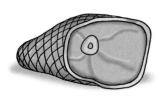
ham
26

fig
27

nut
35

egg
37

milk
71

cake
110

pea
122

bean
123

meat
123

peach
123

rice
125

loaf
130

The number indicates the page on which the word first appears. If a student has difficulty decoding or recognizing a word, refer to that page for more practice.

 roll
135

 corn
139

 flour
146

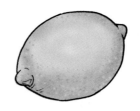 lemon
156

 muffin
158

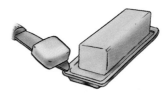 butter
159

 honey
162

 bread
163

 apple
164

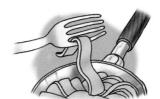 noodle
165

 cheese
175

 orange
176

Plants & Trees

 pine
112

 bush
153

 flower
156

 rose
175

Birds

 jay
128

 crow
131

 owl
147

 eagle
165

Insects

 ant
37

 bee
120

The number indicates the page on which the word first appears. If a student has difficulty decoding or recognizing a word, refer to that page for more practice.

Animals

 fox
74

 skunk
89

 sheep
121

 goat
130

 cow
147

 camel
156

 rabbit
158

 monkey
162

People

 girl
138

 boy
148

tall   taller   tallest

fast   faster   fastest

large   larger   largest

big   bigger   biggest

           g → gg   g → gg

hot   hotter   hottest

          t → tt   t → tt

happy   happier   happiest

          y → i   y → i

heavy   heavier   heaviest

          y → i   y → i

close
shut

ship
boat

shop
store

mad
angry

big
large

little
small

gift
present

bunny
rabbit

shout
yell

over
above

song
tune

sad
unhappy

 hot

 cold

 big

 little

 left

 right

happy

sad

 day

 night

 last

 first

 new

 old

 up

 down

 over

 under

 tall

 short

 pull

 push

 close

 open

Homonyms (Same Sound, Same Spelling)

 fall

 ring

 bat

 fly

 orange

 mouse

 top

 saw

 cut

 right

Homographs (Same Spelling, Different Sounds)

 bow  bow

 wind  wind

 sea

 see

 meat

 meet

 ate

 eight

 write

 right

 rap

 wrap

 flour

 flower

un–  unhappy  unfold

re–  rewrite  return

dis–  disconnect  disappear

–ly  slowly  quickly

–ful  careful  playful

–less  homeless  weightless

 bedroom

 classroom

 lunchroom

 lunchbox

 mailbox

 sandbox

 notebook

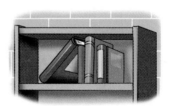 bookshelf

 backpack

 backyard

 raincoat

 rainbow

 snowman

 snowball

 football

 basketball

 sunrise

 sunset

 armchair

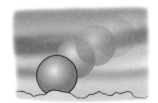 wheelchair

 toothbrush

 toothpaste

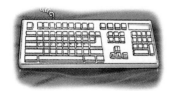 keyboard

 skateboard

 alligator

 hippopotamus

 butterfly

 invitation

 caterpillar

 jellyfish

 dragonfly

 kangaroo

 elevator

 ladybug

 flamingo

 macaroni

 grasshopper

 newspaper

 octopus

 umbrella

 porcupine

 videotape

 quarter

 woodpecker

 refrigerator

 xylophone

 strawberry

 yogurt

 telescope

 zebra

"I'm thinking of an insect that starts with the letter *g* and has three syllables."

"Is it a grasshopper?"

"Yes! That's right!"

I'm thinking of _____
                    an insect / an animal / a bird / a food / an object

that starts with the letter ____ and has

____ syllables.

Students use the words on pages 198–199 to play this word game. The game can also be played with all the categories and words on pages 180–187.

A

 above

 act
actor

 add

 alligator

 alphabet

 angry

 ant

 apple

 arm

 armchair

 ask

B

 baby

 back

 backpack

 backyard

 bad

 bag

 bake
baker

 ball

 band

 bang

 bank

 bark

 barn

 basketball

 bat

 bat

 bath

 bead

 bean

 beat

 bed

 bedroom

 bee

 beetle

 beg

 bell

 belt

 bench

 bend — bent

 best

 bib

 big

 bike

 bird

 bite — bit

 black

 blank

 blanket

 blind

 blink

 block

 blow — blew

 blue

 boat

 bog

 boil

 bolt

 bone

 book

 bookshelf

 boot

 bottom

 bow

 bow

 box

 boy

 brace

 branch

 bread

 breakfast

 brick

 bright

 bring– brought

 broke

 broken

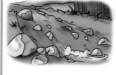 brook

 broom

 brother

 brown

 brush

 bubble

 bud

 bug

 bull

 bump

 bun

 bunk

 bunny

 bus

 bush

 busy

 butter

 butterfly

 button

C

 cabin

 cake

 calf – calves

 call

 camel

 camp

 can

 cane

 cap

 cape

 car

 card

 careful

 cart

 castle

 cat

 catch – caught

 caterpillar

 chain

 chair

 chalk

 check

 cheese

 chop

 clip

 chess

 church

 clock

 chest

 circle

 close

 chick

 clam

 cloud

 chicken

 clap

 clown

 child— children

 class classroom

 club

 chimp

 clay

 coat

 chin

 clean

 cod

 chip

 cliff

coin

 choose

climb

 cold

colt

 colt

 comb

 come

 conduct
conductor

 cone

 cook

 corn

 cot

 cough

 count

 cow

 crab

 cradle

 crank

 crash

 crayon

 crop

 crow

 crust

 cry

 cub

 cube

 cup

 curl

 cut

 cut

 cute

D

 dad

 dam

 dance
dancer

 dinner

 dog

 dark

 dip

 doll

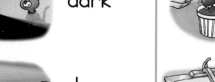 day

 dirty

 dollar

 deer

 disappear

 dolphin

 den

 disconnect

 dome

 dent

 dish

 donkey

 desk

 disk

 door

 dig—
dug

 ditch

 dot

 dime

 dive

 down

 ding dong

 doctor

 dragon

 dragonfly

 draw

 dream

 dress

 drink– drank

 drive– drove

 drop

 drum

 dry

 duck

 duke

 dump

 dune

 dust

 Dutch

E

 eagle

 east

 easy

 eat– ate

 egg

 elephant

 elevator

 elf– elves

 elk

F

 face

 fall– fell

 fall

 fan

 fang

 far

 farm
farmer

 fast

 fat

 father

 feather

 feed —
fed

 fern

 fig

 fill

 fin

 find

 finger

 first

 fish

 fist

 fit

 fix

 flag

 flamingo

 flap

 flat

 flip

 float

 floor

 flour

 flower

 flute

 fly

fly –
flew

fog

foil

fold

follow

foot –
feet

football

fork

fox

frog

fry

full

fun

G

game

gap

gas

gate

get –
got

giant

gift

gill

giraffe

girl

give –
gave

glass

globe

glove

glue

 go—
went

 grow—
grew

 happy

 goat

 gull

 harp

 gold

 gum

 has

 good

H

 hat

 goose—
geese

 half

 have

 graph

 hall

 hay

 grass

 ham

 he

 grasshopper

 hammer

 head

 gray

 hand

 heavy

 green

 hang

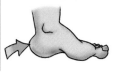 heel

 hen

 herd

 hide

 high

 hike

 hill

 hip

 hippopotamus

 hit

 hive

 hoe

 hog

 hold

 hole

 home

 homeless

 honey

 hook

 hop

 horn

 hose

 hot

 house

 how

 huff

 hug

 hump

 hunt

 hurt

 hut

I

 ice

 ill

 inch

 insect

 invitation

 itch

J

 jacket

 jam

 jar

 jay

 jeep

 jellyfish

 jet

 jig

 job

 jog
jogger

 jug

 jump

 junk

K

 kangaroo

 keyboard

 kick

 kid

 kind

 king

 King Kong

 kiss

 kit

 kite

 kitten

 knee

 knife— knives

 knit

 knock

 L

 lad

 ladder

 ladybug

 lamb

 lamp

 lane

 lap

 large

 last

 laugh

 leaf— leaves

 led

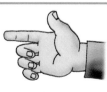 left

 leg

 lemon

 letter

 lift

 light

 lip

 list

 listen

 lit

 little

 loaf—loaves

 lock

 log

 long

 look

 lot

 low

 luck

 lunch

 lunchbox

 lunchroom

M

 macaroni

 mad

 mailbox

 man—men

 mane

 map

 mash

 mask

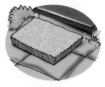 mat

 math

 me

 meal

 meat

 meet—met

 melt

 mend

 middle

milk

 mill

 mitt

 mitten

 mix

 mole

 mom

 money

 monkey

 moon

 mop

 mother

 mouse — mice

 mouse

 mouth

 mud

 muffin

 mug

 mule

 my

N

 name

 nap

 neck

 needle

 nest

 net

 new

 newspaper

 night

 nit

 no

 nod

 none

 noodle

 north

 nose

 not

 note

notebook

 nut

 O

 oar

 octopus

 odd

 off

 oil

 old

 on

 open

 orange

 orange

 our

 oval

 over

 owl

P

 pad

 pail

 paint
painter

 pan

 paper

 park

 patch

 path

 pea

 peach

 peel

 pen

 pencil

 penny — pennies

 pet

 phone

 photo

 pick

 pig

 pillow

 pin

 pinch

 pine

 ping pong

 pink

 pipe

 pit

 pitch

 plane

 planet

 plant

 plate

play

 playful

 please

 point

 pole

 pond

 pony

 poodle

 pool

 pop

 porcupine

 pot

 pour

 present

 press

 princess

 print

 prune

 puddle

 puff

 pull

 pup

 puppet

 puppy— puppies

 purple

 push

 put

 puzzle

Q

 quack

 quarter

 queen

 quick
quickly

 quill

 quilt

 quit

 quiz

R

 rabbit

 race

 raft

 rag

 rain

 rainbow

 raincoat

 rake

 ramp

 ranch

 rap

 rash

 rat

 read

 rectangle

 red

 refrigerator

 rest

 return

 rewrite

 rice

 rich

 ride—
rode

 rig

 right

 right

 ring — rang

 ring

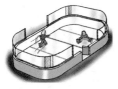 rink

 rip

 road

 roar

 robe

 rock

 rod

 roll

 rose

 round

 row

 rub

 rude

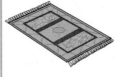 rug

 rule

 ruler

 run — ran

 rut

S

 sack

 sad

 sail

 sand

 sandbox

 sap

 sauce

 save

 saw

 say — said

 score

 scratch

 scream

 sea

 seal

 seat

 see — saw

 seed

 sell — sold

 set

 shadow

 shark

 sharp

 she

 shed

 sheep

 shelf — shelves

 shell

 ship

 shirt

 shop

 shop shopper

 short

 shout

 shovel

 shut

sick

side

sigh

sing—
sang

singer

sink

sip

sister

sit—
sat

skate

 skateboard

 sketch

 skin

 skip

 skirt

 skunk

 sky

 sled

 sleep

sleepy

 sleigh

 slice

 slide

 sling

 slip

 slot

 slowly

 slug

 small

 smart

 smell

 smog

 smoke

 snake

 sneaker

 snow

 snowball

 snowman

 soap

 sob

 sock

 soil

 some

 song

 soup

 south

 space

 spell

 spider

 spill

 spin

 splash

 split

 spoon

 spot

 spray

 spring

 square

 squirrel

 stamp

 stand

 star

 steeple

 stem

 step

 stick

 sting

 stink

 stir

 stole

 stool

 stop

 store

 storm

 stove

 straw

 strawberry

 street

 stretch

 string

 study

 sub

 summer

 sun

 sunrise

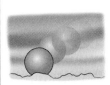 sunset

 supper

 swap

 sweater

 sweep

 swim
swimmer

 swing

 switch

T

 table

 tag

 tail

 talk

 tall

 tan

 tank

 tap

 tape

 teach –
taught

 teacher

 team

 teeth

 telescope

 tell –
told

 tent

 test

 thank

 that

 these

 thick

 thin

 thing

 think –
thought

 this

 those

thread	 toll	 track
 throw – threw	 took	 tractor
thumb	 tooth	 train
 tick	toothbrush	 trap
 tickle	toothpaste	 trash
 time	top	 tree
 tiny	top	 triangle
 tip	tot	 trick
 toad	 town	 trot
toe	 toy	 truck

 trunk

 tub

 tube

 tug

 tune

 turn

 turtle

U

 umbrella

 under

 unfold

 unhappy

 up

 us

V

 van

 vat

 vest

 vet

 videotape

 vote

W

 wag

 wagon

 walk

 wall

 was

 watch

 wax

 we

 weather

 wheat

 wind
windy

 weigh

 wheel

 wind

 weight

 wheelchair

 window

 weightless

 when

 wing

 well

 which

 wink

 went

 white

 winter

 were

 why

 wipe

 west

 wig

 wish

 wet

 wild

 with

 whale

 win
winner

 wolf—
wolves

woman—women

 wood

 woodpecker

 wool

 work

 wrap

 wrist

write

wrong

 X

 xylophone

Y

 yam

 yard

 yarn

 yell

 yellow

yo-yo

 yogurt

 you

Z

 zebra

 zip

 zipper

 zit

 zoo

NUMBERS

1	one	11	eleven	20	twenty
2	two	12	twelve	30	thirty
3	three	13	thirteen	40	forty
4	four	14	fourteen	50	fifty
5	five	15	fifteen	60	sixty
6	six	16	sixteen	70	seventy
7	seven	17	seventeen	80	eighty
8	eight	18	eighteen	90	ninety
9	nine	19	nineteen	100	one hundred
10	ten				

DAYS

SUN	Sun.	Sunday
MON	Mon.	Monday
TUE	Tues.	Tuesday
WED	Wed.	Wednesday
THU	Thurs.	Thursday
FRI	Fri.	Friday
SAT	Sat.	Saturday

MONTHS

JAN	Jan.	January
FEB	Feb.	February
MAR	Mar.	March
APR	Apr.	April
MAY	May	May
JUN	June	June
JUL	July	July
AUG	Aug.	August
SEP	Sept.	September
OCT	Oct.	October
NOV	Nov.	November
DEC	Dec.	December

PLACES & ABBREVIATIONS

Ave.	Avenue
Blvd.	Boulevard
Fwy.	Freeway
Hwy.	Highway
Pl.	Place
Rd.	Road
St.	Street
Tpk.	Turnpike
N.	North
S.	South
E.	East
W.	West

TITLES & ABBREVIATIONS

For a man:
Mr.

For a woman:
Miss
Ms.
Mrs.

Numbers indicate the pages on which words appear. (Review lessons are not included in this listing.)